david
horvitz

change the name of the days

The original project, 32 mailed lessons, emerged from David Horvitz's unexpectedly long-distance residency at Nassauischer Kunstverein Wiesbaden initiated by his reception of the Follow Fluxus 2020 prize, awarded by the Hessian State Capital of Wiesbaden and the Nassauischer Kunstverein Wiesbaden.

ISBN 978-2-36568-053-0

david
horvitz

change the name of the days

JBE BOOKS & YVON LAMBERT

ELA

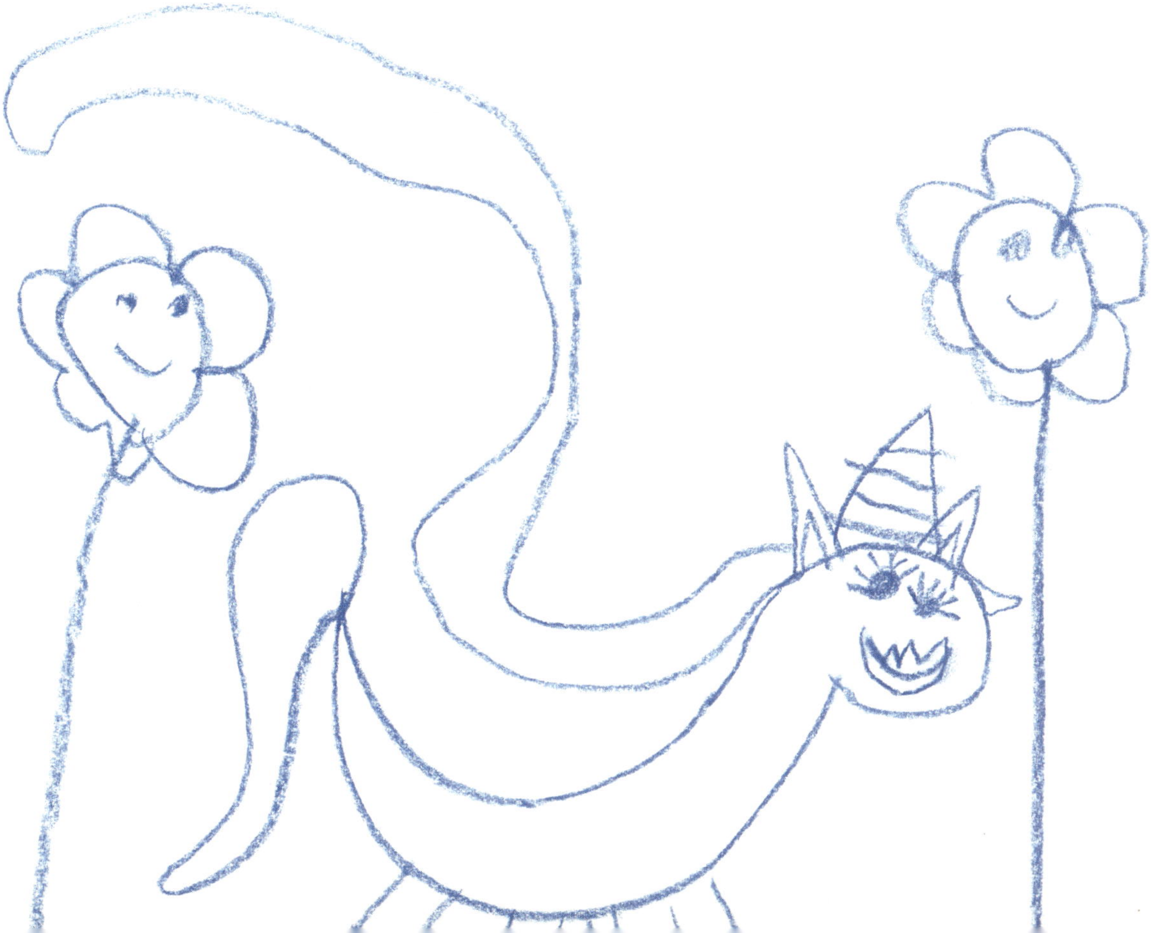

David Horvitz's *Epistolichory*
by Natilee Harren

Dear student,

This book contains 32 lessons written by the artist David Horvitz. Altogether they make a curriculum of daily activities that anyone can do: kids, parents, or even adult children (as the artist would say). David wrote them during a time when most people couldn't go to work or school, and some people couldn't even leave their homes. He first started to write them for his daughter Ela, who, like many other children, was home from school. But then he thought the lessons might be useful for others too. So, each week for 32 weeks (from October 2020 to May 2021), he typed out a lesson (arranging the words in an interesting way), printed it out in 100 copies (using a rainbow of colored paper), and sent it to friends through the mail. More people wanted to receive the lessons, so he added those people, too. At the end of 32 weeks, about 120 people were receiving David's lessons. A curriculum like this one is a set of activities to follow, almost like a walking trail. If you finish all the lessons, by the end you will have completed a course, and you will likely be a different kind of person than you were at the beginning. Maybe you can even begin to teach your lessons to others.

David's first lesson is to "Make a drawing the length of a minute." You might think this instruction is easy to do, but then David asks you a bunch of questions: "What is a minute? How long is a minute? How long is your minute? Can two different people have two different minutes? Who says how long it is?" Now you might be confused. But the trick is just to draw your minute and see what happens. Then you will know the answer to these questions. Even better, draw your minute with a friend. Because then you will have two drawings, two minutes, and two sets of answers to David's questions. There is always more than one answer, more than one way to do things.

You will see that David invites us to do many different kinds of things: make, look, find, grow, learn, change, enter, walk, draw, carry, try, welcome, exchange, ask, displace, invent, guide, adjust, plant, count, transcribe, pronounce, resonate, give. He tells us to write, draw, and paint. To make photographs and sounds. To make marks and maps. David's lessons ask us to notice other things and other beings, like plants and trees, the wind, water (sometimes puddles, sometimes a river), a cat or a crow, or someone else, whoever that someone may be. They may seem simple, but they invite us to pay attention with our whole mind, and without prejudice, to all that we do. These are the artist's lessons.

Many of David's lessons are about nature, but many are about human culture. Things like words, holidays, time, or the rules we all agree to follow as a community or a society. In fact, his instructions often invite us to change the ways we think about nature and culture together. Does our culture control how we appreciate nature? What if we reimagined our culture to better fit nature? For example, "Change the name of the days" (also the name of this book) is one of David's lessons. It's about the names we give to the alternating periods of light and dark that organize our lives and that are actually controlled by nature's Earth, sun, and moon. David has said, "I want to believe that we can each have our own time—or that we can purposefully fall out of sync with the time of clocks and calendars."

If we change the name of the days, we might un-learn the day names we were taught in school. But David thinks we will also learn something else, something new. And this something will better reflect who and where we are in the world. This is a lesson that David has been thinking about for a long time, and he invites you to think about it too, because changing the names of the days changes the way we think about and experience them. In that sense, David's lessons are about the transformative power of perception. If you change the way you think about the days, you are, in reality, changing your days. If you change the way you think about the world, you will change your world.

In the past, other artists have also experimented with writing lessons, such as the artists who worked together in the 1960s and '70s under the name Fluxus. They wrote instructions like "Please wash your face" (Benjamin Patterson); "Draw a straight line and follow it" (La Monte Young); "Light a match and watch till it goes out" (Yoko Ono); or "Scream!! Scream!! Scream!! Scream!! Scream!! Scream!!" (Dick Higgins). You might try some of these if you like. The Fluxus artist Robert Filliou thought of works like these as "mind openers," much like David's lessons are. David's lessons particularly evoke the example of artists like Alison Knowles, Pauline Oliveros, and Mieko Shiomi, who wrote instructions almost like recipes, created with the ingredients of everyday life. Their instructions use activities and objects that we often use when spending time with other people and caring for them.

In 2020, David was awarded the Follow Fluxus award by the Nassauischer Kunstverein in Wiesbaden, Germany, the city where Fluxus started. He was supposed to have an exhibition and residency there but he couldn't go, because the world was closed. So, he sent his lessons there and elsewhere and invited other people—the students of the lessons in this book—to send documentation of their activities to the gallery instead. In a sense, the exhibition happened wherever people tried out David's lessons. Robert Filliou would have called this an example of "The Eternal Network." Anyone can join, can form their own center, no matter where (or when) they are.

Like Fluxus, conceptual artists who have made art out of ideas, like Lawrence Weiner and Robert Barry, use language to make their work. Oftentimes, you don't even have to act out their instructions. Thinking about them is enough. The minimal poet Aram Saroyan, who happens to be David's neighbor, also makes art with language and ideas. But it is important that you see his words directly on the page, because the way his poems appear impacts how we understand them. For instance:

lighght

is a single-word, visual poem by Aram Saroyan. Of course, one of the exciting things about David's lessons is that we don't always know what is going to happen when we try them out. In that way, they recall the music of composer John Cage, who was interested in chance, or indeterminacy. For instance, sometimes John Cage would flip a coin to decide which note to play next.

Above all, David's interest in chance is rooted in nature. That is why it's helpful to think of his lessons as seeds. As it happens, in early November 2020, he mailed out an actual seed (a beautiful pea seed he found at a corner florist in Lisbon) with the instruction, "Grow a magic bean to bring down the giant." If you visit David's house or the studio where he makes his art, you will see plants everywhere. There is an ever-expanding village of potted plants in all sizes, multiplying across corners, countertops, and the sidewalk outside. He is constantly collecting seeds to bring home to germinate, and he also takes seeds from his collection and disperses them as he travels. He likes to plant seeds where people don't care to see things grow, like in the cracks of sidewalks, across concrete-strewn vacant lots, or (at least one time) throughout the pristinely manicured golf course of a certain giant (who, as it turned out, did fall from the sky quite recently). When seeds are dispersed by the wind it is called *anemochory*. When they travel by water it is *hydrochory*. By animals, *zoochory*. There is not yet an established word for this, but when seeds travel by mail, as they have through David's lessons, maybe we could call it *epistolichory*. Anyway, David works this way because he thinks that, like a depleting landscape, our attention spans have "eroded." To combat this, he is interested in "forms of meditation that cultivate the enjoyment of time."

David often talks about his artworks as if it they were seeds *broadcast*, or cast at random into the world, and he thinks of the places where his art goes as sites for those seeds to be planted, to *germinate*, to grow into a garden, and eventually to *propagate* on their own. These words are important to his practice. So, as yet another lesson, I include their definitions here:

broadcast, verb
to cast or throw seed in all directions, as from the hand in sowing

germinate, verb
to cause to sprout

propagate, verb
to be produced or multiplied by generation, or by new shoots or plants

Ultimately, David's lessons teach us that anywhere you find a patch of dirt—a bit of space and time dedicated for the purpose of growth—there can be a garden. Anyone who holds this book of lessons holds the tools to shift their thinking, to change their mind, transform their consciousness, and maybe even their world.

What is a minute? How long is a minute? How long is your minute? Can you make a minute longer? Can you make it shorter? Can two different people have two different minutes? Who says how long it is? Make a continuous drawing for the duration of one minute. Look at other people's minutes. See how each one is different. Each drawing is both a mark of time (your time) and a map of your movement.

1

make
a
drawing
the
length
of a
minute

What does it mean to know a place? To be familiar with a place? How well do you know your home? Your neighborhood? Your town? In a place that you know, look for something that you don't know. For something you never knew was there. For something you may have looked at everyday but never really looked at.

in a familiar place look for the unfamiliar

2

What story does a tree tell? Can you hear its words vibrating in the air? Can you read its words written on its leaves? Do you understand its language? Collect the leaves of a tree or of many trees. Bind them together with string or something else to make a book. Read the story. Read it aloud to others.

3

make
a
book
written
by
a
tree

Make a photograph of someone who is not here. Or of someone who is no longer here. Or who was never here. Or who has left. Or who cannot arrive. Maybe someone close by but out of sight. Or faraway. Someone on the other side of a continent, an ocean, a river, a wall. Or maybe someone who is no longer living. Try to represent them with a photograph. Or simply point the camera in the direction that they are and take a picture. Print the photograph. On or under the photograph, write their name.

4

make a
photograph
of
someone
who
is
not
here

Find where a river once was. Or maybe a stream. Or a creek. Maybe it is buried under the asphalt street and still flows underground. Or underneath the cement sidewalk. Maybe it is in the city gutters. Look for its traces that may still exist: puddles, erosion, plants growing from a hidden water source. Walk its path as if you were moving water, moving towards the sea. Walk as if you were making a drawing across the grid of the city. Make the sounds of water and think about what else is buried underneath your feet. If it can be remembered, say its name.

5

find a buried river

Find a magic bean to grow. Listen to or read the story of Jack and the Beanstalk and germinate the magic bean at home. Think about how with the right conditions - warmth and moisture - this little seed will begin to grow and will help you defeat the giant. Think about how one little action can spread out like ripples across water.

6

grow
a
magic bean
to bring down
the giant

On the ground, in chalk, write the names of faraway places. Inscribe somewhere with somewhere else. Learn to spell places where you are not. Learn to spell where you are not. Write them where you walk. Imagine you are renaming the ground. Imagine you are walking in the other place. Make two places touch. Make two places meet. Inscribe somewhere with somewhere else.

In Wiesbaden, write California write Iceland write Paris write Kyoto write Istanbul write London write Beirut write Milan. Write California not in California. In California, write not California.

7

learn to write the names of places

Why do the days have names? What do they mean? Who named them? Why are there seven days in a week? Can there be more? Can there be less? In some places, there were more. And less. In some places, each day had two names. Think about what the days' names mean. Now change their names. Maybe Monday is foxday. Sunday is cheeseday. Wednesday is kjefijeadjiday. If you want, change the number of days of the week as well. Now try to live each day using the new names and try to forget the old names. If you changed the number of days in the week, try to live on this new week.

8

change

the

n a m e

of

the

d a y s

Pour a glass of tap water onto the ground to make a small puddle. Watch the shape it makes. Imagine this is a painting. A painting that disappears. Watch it disappear as it evaporates. As it evaporates imagine where it goes. Into the air, into a cloud, into rain, into sea, into a wave crashing against the shore on some faraway beach. Then evaporated again, into fog, dripped into a river, into the tap water in your house, then into you when you drink it. Now think about where the water came from that you just poured. How did it get to your faucet? Where did it come from? What distance did it travel? Make photographs of the puddle (your painting) until it disappears.

9

make a puddle

Crows and ravens and magpies and other corvids are some of the smartest birds. They are known to remember the faces of people. And sometimes, to those they are amicable with, they even offer gifts. Today's lesson is simple yet complex. To enter into the memory of a bird. Imagine memory as a place you can enter into. Or a story you can become a character of. Talk to the crows near you. Learn to speak their language. Give them food to eat. Over time (and this may take some time) they will begin to recognize your actions. You will become familiar to them. You will be remembered by them. Maybe you will receive a gift.

10

enter

the memory of a crow

Walk towards the moon. Walk in the direction of the moon. Follow the moon. Orient yourself with the moon. Tread a path to the moon. Imagine you are on a street that moves with the moon's moves. If you are in an open field you can do this as a straight line. If you are in a city, walk as straight as you can against the city's grid - against the straight lines of the streets and blocks. Imagine a city that lined up with the moon. You will walk with no destination except where you end up when you follow the moon.

11

walk in a line

towards the moon

Draw a unicorn wherever you go. As my daughter lay falling asleep in her half dream-state she told me a stream of new lessons/instructions/actions/scores that she wanted me to write. This was one of them. She asks that you draw it in chalk. Take a photograph of it. Put the photograph up on your wall.

12

draw a unicorn wherever you go

Memorize a sentence and try to carry it across the night and through your dreams. Say it out loud when you go to sleep and say it out loud when you wake up in the morning. If you can remember it in your dreams, say it to yourself while you are dreaming. If you need a sentence, here is one to use by Clarice Lispector: "We make it with our breaths together."

13

carry

a

sentence

across

the

night

This is another one Ela told me. It is important to look at clouds.

14

look
at
the
sky
and
see
if
you
can
see
a
picture
in
the
clouds

Ela said this just before falling asleep. You can ask her what it means.

15

try to smell another world and it might look like your world

If you live in a city, you might live in a place that has forgotten about the night. After the sun has set, the day lingers artificially. The French call dusk, the time right after the sun sets, as "between the dog and the wolf" (entre chien et loup). But streetlights and lightbulbs resist nightfall and the dog keeps the wolf away. It never gets truly dark anymore. And most stars get lost in the haze of light pollution above us.

This lesson is simple. At night, keep all the lights off in your house. In your house try to experience the darkness of night. Imagine a time long ago when at nightfall, the only light we would see would be the lingering light on the horizon of the no-longer-visible sun, the moon, or stars, maybe a fire or candle, some fireflies, or possibly glowing mushrooms or algae in the sea. Keep the lights off all night. Do this for a night or a week or a month or a year. Welcome the night into your house.

16

welcome the night into your house

When you breathe, you are breathing a plant's breath. When a plant breathes, it is breathing your breath. It is a reciprocal relationship, an economy of gifts, a sharing of air. Find a plant. Maybe in your house or outside. It can be a giant tree or the smallest weed. Sit for a short time and breathe with it.

17

exchange

breaths

with

a

plant

It is said that ninjas in Japan could tell the time by looking into the eyes of a cat. This was because the shape of the cat's pupil changed at different times of the day, following the sun across the sky. Find a cat and look in its eyes to see what time it is. When you need to know the time again later, ask the cat again. Ask your parents if they will replace all their clocks with cats.

18

ask a cat for the time

Look at the rocks around you. How did they get there? How old are they? Some rocks were moved by people. Like those smooth stones decorating the outsides of buildings. They were put there by people. They are from ancient rivers found underground. Others, like giant rocks in a natural landscape, those may have been pushed there by glaciers millions of years ago. You will move your own rock. Pick up a small rock. Feel its shape and weight and texture in your hand. Imagine how old it must be. Then carry it in your pocket with you. When you've found a nice place for it, leave it there. (The artist Lygia Clark would give stones to people to remind them of what is real.)

19

displace

a

rock

minutely

What is a holiday? How many holidays are in the year? Is today a holiday? Was today a holiday? There used to be more holidays than there are now. Many were removed from the calendar to make more days for work and discipline and less for play and celebration. For this lesson, invent your own holiday. It could be for any reason. What rituals will you do? What will you eat? What is its date? Is it just one day or many days? Give the holiday a name and don't forget the date for next year!

20

invent your own holiday

This is for two people. It is a listening walk. One person will close their eyes. The other will guide the closed-eyes person on a walk safely through a landscape. This can be anywhere. In a city, on a beach, in a forest, inside a grocery store. The person whose eyes are closed will listen to the sounds around them. When the walk is done, switch places and repeat. Imagine the sounds you hear are a composition of music. (The composer Pauline Oliveros asks us to listen with our feet when we walk.)

guid 2l e

someone

through

the

sounds

around

you

When you enter a body of water your body raises the water level through displacement. Like when you get in a bath and the water goes over the edge. Next time you are at the beach, enter into the ocean with the intention of infinitesimally raising the level of the sea. Imagine this imperceptible change that you caused. Now exit the water returning the sea level back to what it was.

22

adjust the level of the sea

Pour water on the ground outside until a puddle is formed and there is a reflection in the puddle and you can see the sky. Look down to look up.

make a puddle

#2

What does it mean for something to have a name? How does your relationship to it change? How does your awareness shift through its familiarization? Go outside and name a tree.

24

give a tree a name

Make the city into a musical instrument. Play it. Perform it. Pound the sidewalk like a drum. Sound the lamp posts like bells. Resonate buildings and cars like giant accordions. Bang on signs like gongs. Make music. Make music everywhere!

resonate the city

25

Find the boundary between here and there and draw it out on the ground. You can draw it with chalk or pebbles or string or anything.

26

make a line between here and there

Write your name in the ground using seeds. This can be small, on a tiny piece of dirt, or huge across a giant field. Water the seeds or forget about them and let the rain water them. Let your name grow into a garden. Let your name blossom into flowers and then seed into seeds. Let the birds take away your name as seeds letting your name be planted across the planet's surface becoming indecipherable. Write your name on the planet's surface.

27

plant
your
name
in
the
earth

Usually when someone asks you how old you are, you tell them the answer in years. Maybe you are 5 years old. Or 6 years old. Or maybe you are 5 ½ or 6 ¼ years old. But your age can be defined in other ways of counting. Maybe think of your age in days. Or weeks or months or hours or seconds. As I write this I am 14,161 days old. Or 2,023 weeks old. Or 339,864 hours old. How old are you?

28

c o u n t y o u r d a y s' a g e

Listen to the wind. Listen to the nuances of its sounds, of its language. Where has it been? What has it seen? Where is it going? Imagine it is telling you a story of its journey. Transcribe its sounds to paper. You can use your alphabet or invent a new alphabet for the wind. (In your alphabet it might look like this: wooohhhhhhhhhwohhhh woohhhhhhhhhwwwwwwwwwhhhoooh-hhhhh wssshhhhhhhhhhhhhhhhhhhsshhhhsshhhhhhshssshhhhhhhshshhshshshwwwws-shhhhwhwhwhwhwhwhhhwwhwhhshssshhhhhssshhshshwwwwwwwshhhhhhssshh-hssshshshshshshshshshhsssh.) After you've written it down, perform it for others.

29

t r anscribe
the
s o unds
of
the
w i nd

If you have ever traveled, you might have noticed that the same word sounds different in different places. The word "water" sounds different in Los Angeles than in London. Or the word "coyote" spoken in different places in the United States. Also the same word might even change slightly in different languages. Like ocean in English or océan in French or oceano in Italian, Spanish, or Portuguese. Sounds change in different places. Accents and dialects respond to local geographies. Pick a word and change the way it sounds. Make a new local dialect for where you live.

pronounce

a word

in

a new

way

30

Invent a new kind of money. Maybe it is pebbles, sticks, rain drops, cat hair, leaves, paper clips, sea shells, sounds, breaths, strings, feathers, seeds, sand, cups of tea, cups of coffee... Really, anything. Now start to use this new form of money with your friends.

31

make
new
money

This is the last instruction. You can invent your own idea. Write it on the paper.

32

David Horvitz is an artist, living with his daughter Ela Melanie in Los Angeles. Sometimes they change the name of the days. Sometimes they look at the sky. Sometimes they make a photograph of someone who is not here. Sometimes they walk toward the moon. Sometimes they welcome the night into their house. Sometimes they ask a cat for the time. Sometimes they give a tree a name. Sometimes they transcribe the sounds of the wind.

Natilee Harren is a critic and scholar of modern and contemporary art history and theory, with a particular focus on experimental, interdisciplinary practices after 1960. She teaches at the University of Houston School of Art.

This book is the third volume in the collection JBE <3 Kids
Directed by Mathieu Cénac and David Desrimais
Assisted by Milène Josse
Co-published with Yvon Lambert

Layout
Emma Zampieri—Studio JBE

Typeface
Minion Pro

Proofreading
Monique Gross
Cassandra Katsiaficas

Photoengraving
IGS Print

The authors and editors would like to thank
Aure Bergeret
Samantha Calteau
Hélène & Pierre Cénac
Jenny Chert & Florian Lüdde
Jisoo Chung
Pierre-Édouard Couton
Didier Desrimais
Zanna Gilbert
Elke Gruhn
Benjamin Hélion
Ela Melanie Horvitz
Damien Jacq
Ève Lambert
Yvon Lambert
Benjamin Lanot
Bruno Mayrargue
Michael G. Powell
Olivia de Smedt
Woosung Sohn
Ben Wolfson
Kunstverein Wiesbaden
USPS

Jean Boîte Éditions
51 rue Claude Decaen
75012 Paris
jbe-books.com

Yvon Lambert
14 Rue des Filles du Calvaire
75003 Paris
yvon-lambert.com

ISBN: 978-2-36568-053-0
Legal deposit: June 2021
First edition

Printed in Lithuania